Facts About the Ringneck Pheasant

By Lisa Strattin

© 2016 Lisa Strattin

Revised © 2019

Facts for Kids Picture Books by Lisa Strattin

Harlequin Macaw, Vol 34

Downy Woodpecker, Vol 37

Frilled Lizard, Vol 39

Purple Finch, Vol 48

Poison Dart Frogs, Vol 50

Giant Otter, Vol 57

Hornbill, Vol 67

Dwarf Lemur, Vol 73

Giant Squirrel, Vol 76

Star Tortoise, Vol 79

Sign Up for New Release Emails Here

http://LisaStrattin.com/subscribe-here

Monthly Surprise Box

http://KidCraftsByLisa.com

All rights reserved. No part of this book may be reproduced by any means whatsoever without the written permission from the author, except brief portions quoted for purpose of review.

All information in this book has been carefully researched and checked for factual accuracy. However, the author and publisher makes no warranty, express or implied, that the information contained herein is appropriate for every individual, situation or purpose and assume no responsibility for errors or omissions. The reader assumes the risk and full responsibility for all actions, and the author will not be held responsible for any loss or damage, whether consequential, incidental, special or otherwise, that may result from the information presented in this book.

All images are free for use or purchased from stock photo sites for commercial use.

Some coloring pages might be of the general species due to lack of available images.

I have relied on my own observations as well as many different sources for this book and I have done my best to check facts and give credit where it is due. In the event that any material is used without proper permission, please contact me so that the oversight can be corrected.

Contents

INTRODUCTION 7

CHARACTERISTICS 9

APPEARANCE 11

LIFE STAGES 13

LIFE SPAN 15

SIZE 17

HABITAT 19

DIET 21

FRIENDS AND ENEMIES 23

SUITABILITY AS PETS 25

RINGNECK PHEASANT PHOTO 38

MONTHLY SURPRISE BOX 39

INTRODUCTION

Ringneck pheasants are native to Europe and Asia. They have been introduced to many other countries and can be found throughout the United States. They prefer to live in open areas like fields, but can live anywhere.

They are a medium sized bird that is often hunted. They are dark colored and have long necks and tails. They spend most of their time on the ground and very little time flying.

Ringneck peasants are very social birds. They will feed and hang out in large flocks. They also flock during the mating season with one male flocking with several females.

They are omnivorous and eat plant material and insects. They have many enemies as they have a negative impact on native birds in the United States. They can be particular harmful to lesser prairie chickens, which are a threatened bird.

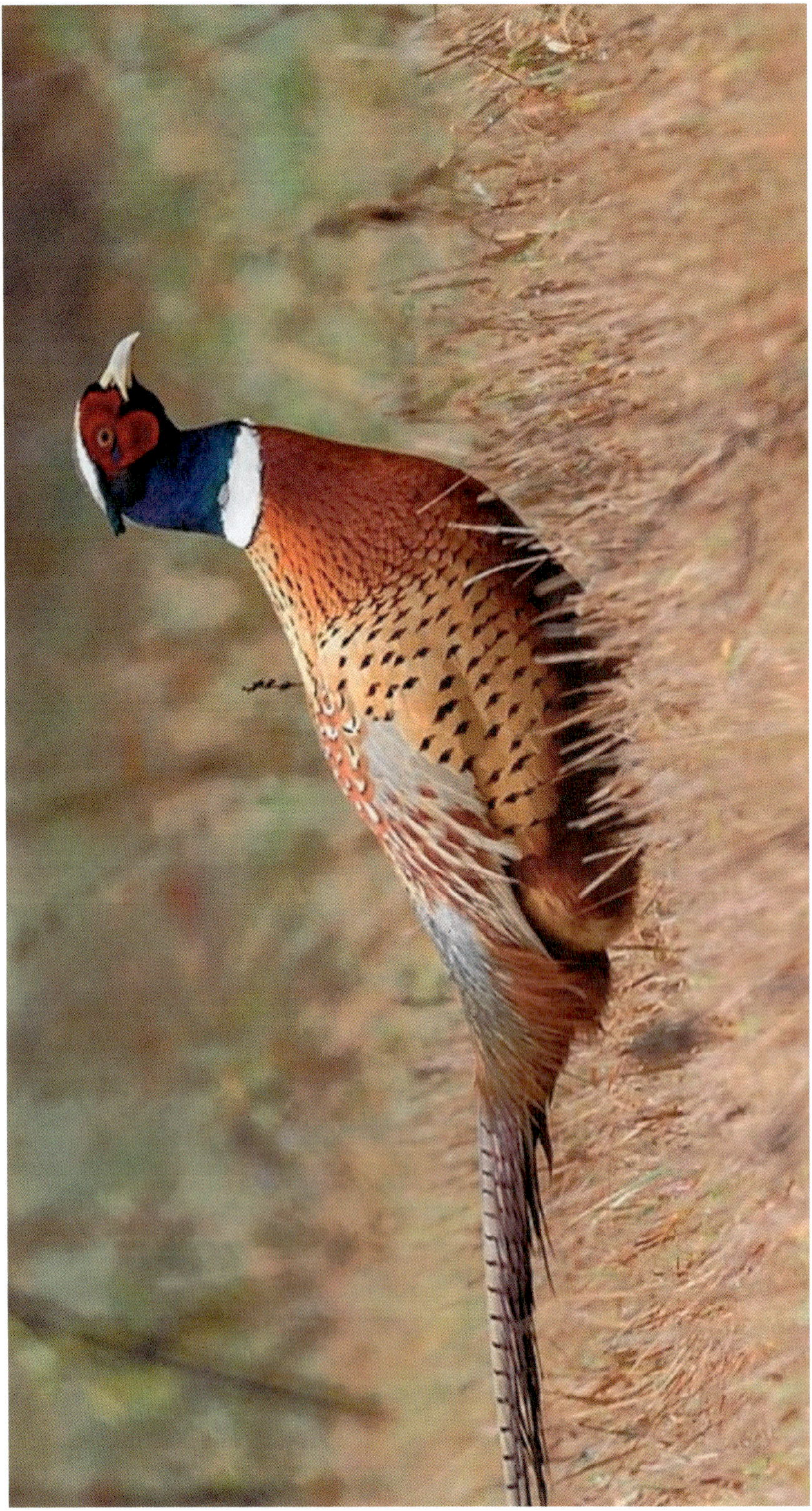

CHARACTERISTICS

Ringneck pheasants are frequently grown on farms to be released for hunting. They are one of the most popular birds to hunt in the United Kingdom. They have also been introduced to the United States for hunting purposes.

During the winter, their flocks are usually mixed of males and females. However, in the spring these flocks usually only have one male with several females. This is the beginning of the mating season.

Ringneck pheasants can run very well and spend the majority of their time on the ground. They do roost in trees sometimes, but they also roost on the ground.

They are very strong fliers and can take off almost vertically when they are spooked. They bathe by taking dust baths. This helps them remove dry skin and helps them to get rid of old feathers.

10

APPEARANCE

Male ringneck pheasants are more colorful than the females. This helps female pheasants to blend into their surroundings when they are incubating their nests. Male pheasants have long, barred, and pointed tales and bright red eye patches. The males also have a white ring that goes around their necks. This is how they get their name! Females are a dull brown to black color.

Males are larger than the females. They stand taller and have a much longer tail than compared to females.

12

LIFE STAGES

Ringneck pheasants have three life stages. The first life stage is the egg. This life stage begins during mating season when the female lays seven to 15 eggs in a nest dug in the ground, and lined with plant material. The eggs hatch in 23 to 28 days. After they hatch the second life stage begins.

The juvenile stage is the second life stage. When they hatch, juveniles are covered in feathers and are able to follow their mothers to food sources. Juveniles will stay with their mothers for 70 to 80 days before they are on their own. They will reach the adult life stage in one year. Adulthood is the final life stage.

14

LIFE SPAN

Ringneck pheasants do not have very long life spans. In the wild, most juvenile birds do not survive into Autumn and it is very rare for adult pheasants to live more than three years. They have many enemies that make it hard for them to survive very long.

Captive ringneck pheasants live much longer and can live 11 to 18 years. This is due to their decreased risk of attack from enemies while in captivity.

16

SIZE

Ringneck pheasants weigh two to three pounds, are 16 to 22 inches long, and have a wingspan of nine to 11 inches. Males tend to have much longer tails than the females do.

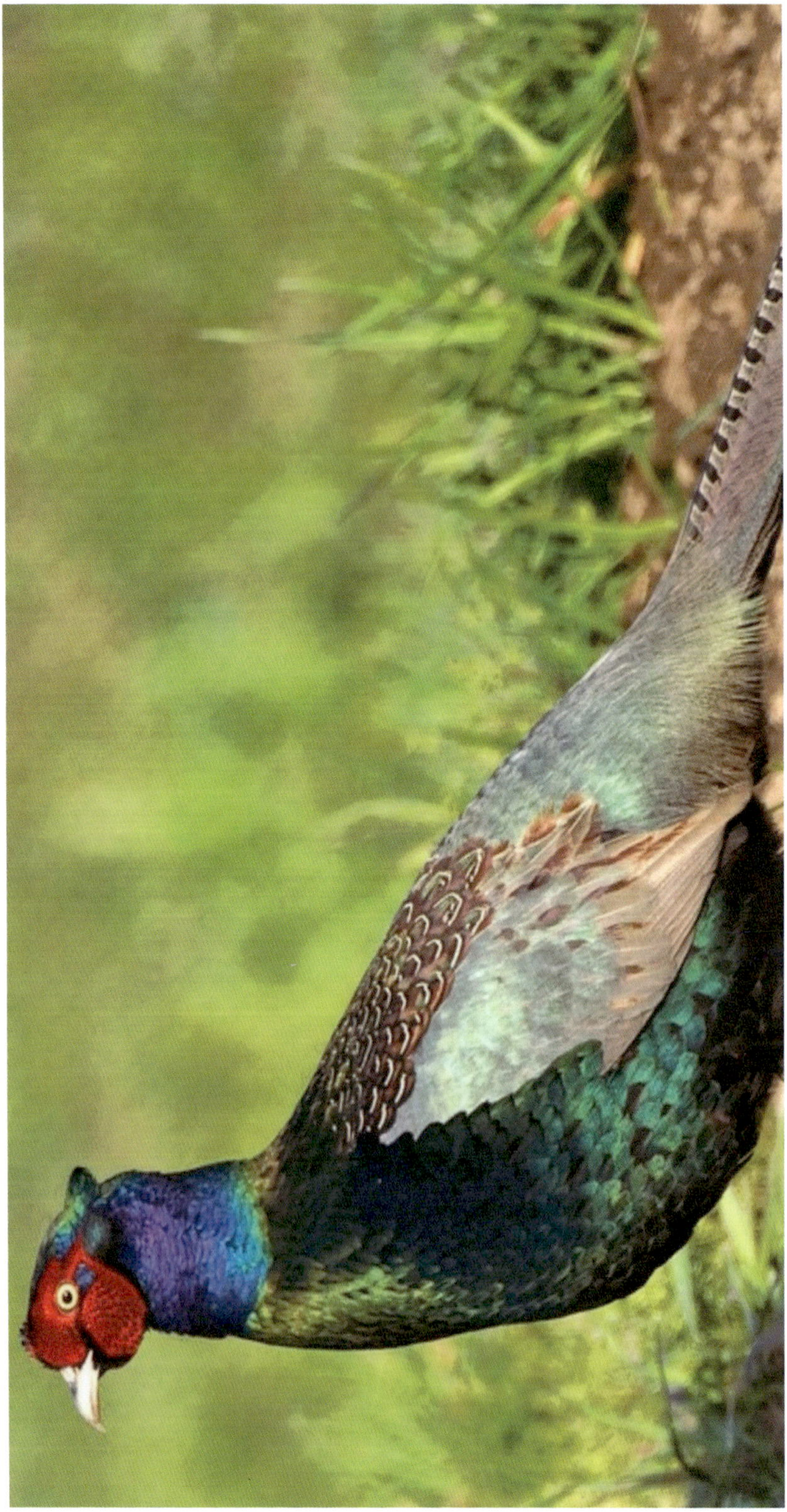

HABITAT

Ringneck pheasants are able to adapt to many types of habitats. They prefer more open areas, such as fields and pastures. This environment allows them to see their enemies and they can quickly escape if they are threatened. They will also live in areas that are heavily forested. These areas usually have a lot of ground cover, which is a key component of their habitat. This helps them to hide their nests and make it harder for their enemies to find them. They also use this cover to protect juvenile birds, who are not able to run as fast as adults, by hiding them. Furthermore, adult pheasants will use this cover to escape their enemies.

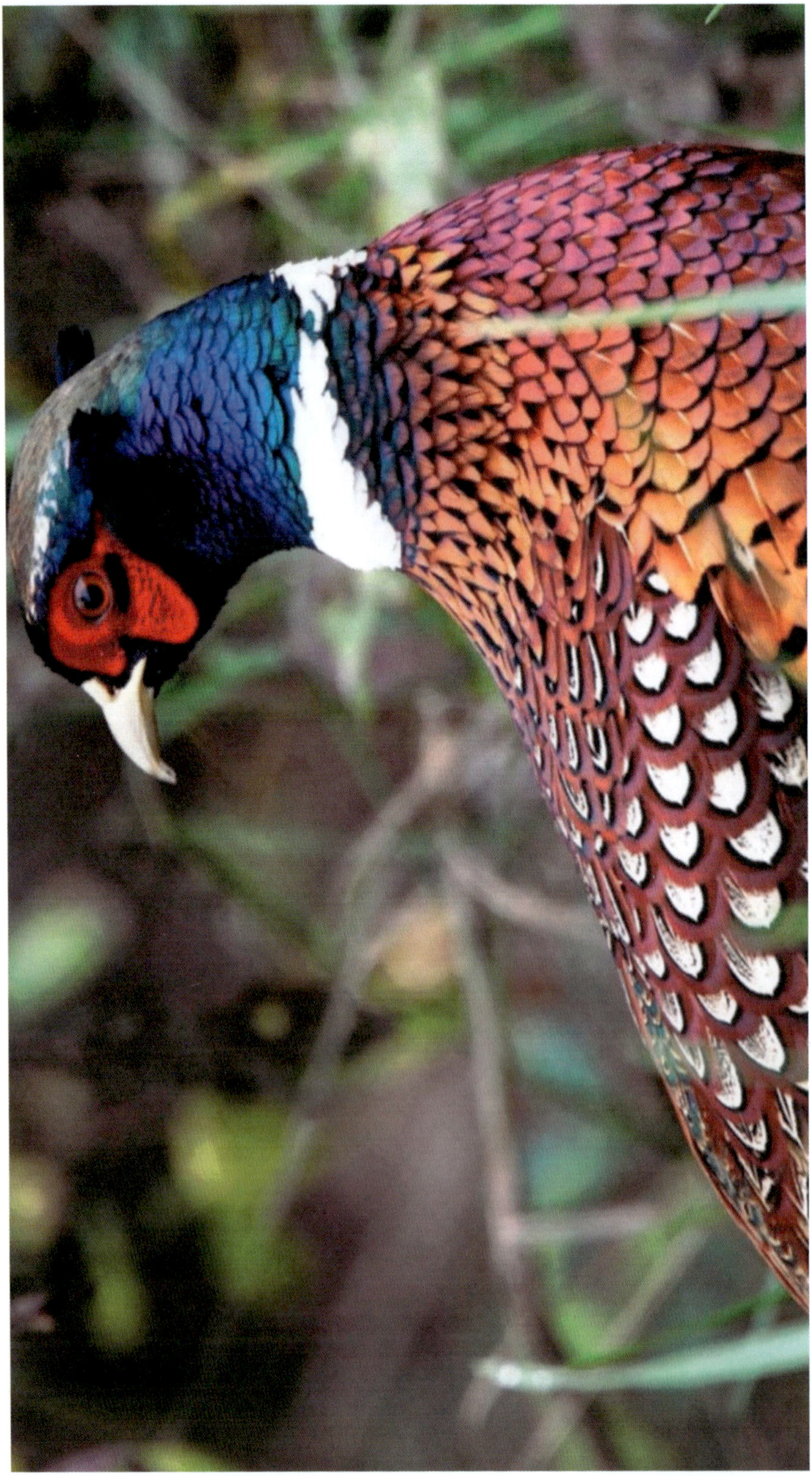

DIET

Ringneck pheasants are omnivorous and will eat most types of food. They will eat agricultural crops and like corn, wheat, barley, and flax. They also eat seeds from wild plants and prefer foxtail, ragweed, and sunflower seeds. They eat apples, wild grapes, and blackberries. They also like to eat insects and feed on crickets and grasshoppers. They eat a lot of different things!

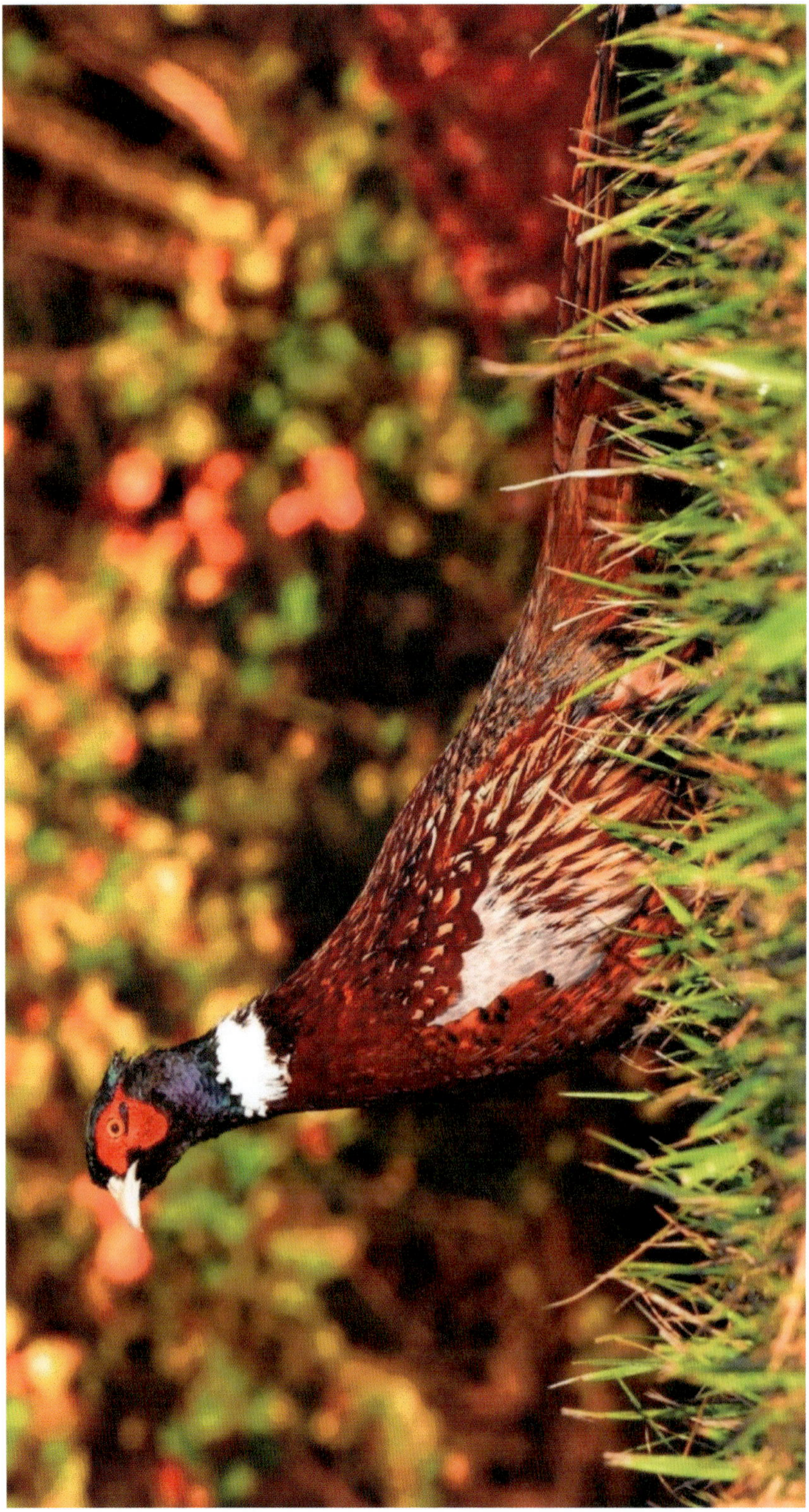

FRIENDS AND ENEMIES

Ringneck pheasants are very social birds and are friends with other ringneck pheasants. They gather in large flocks to feed and roost. This helps them keep an eye out for their enemies and help reduce the chance of being attacked.

They have many enemies. Foxes, domestic dogs, domestic cats, coyotes, hawks, bobcats, owls, skunks, and opossums are all enemies of pheasants. These enemies will attack all life stages of pheasants. Pheasants are also enemies with native bird species in places where they have been introduced. In the United States, pheasants outcompete native bird species, like the lesser prairie chicken. Pheasants will eat food and use habitats that are important for the prairie chicken, making it hard for the prairie chicken to survive in areas where the pheasants live.

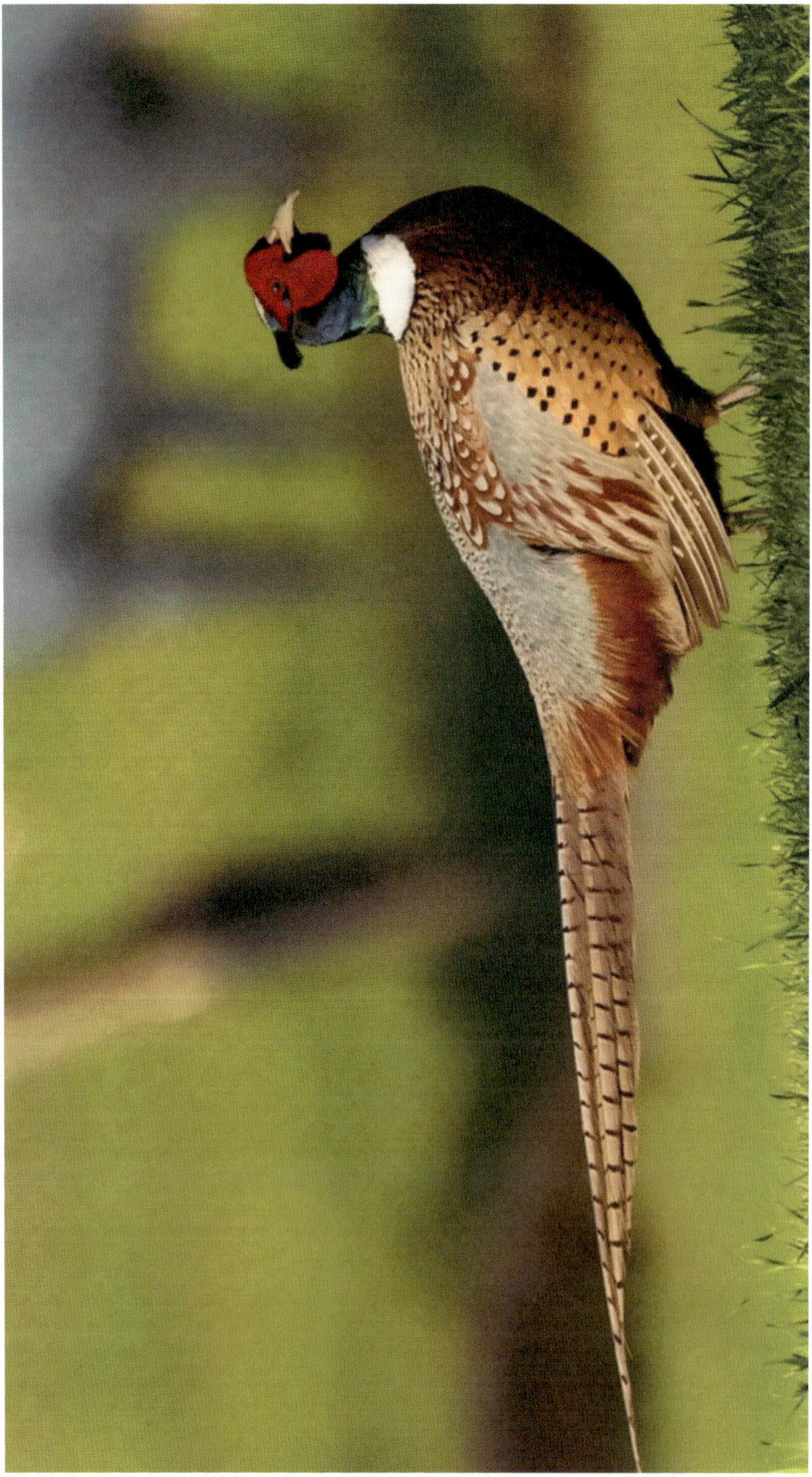

SUITABILITY AS PETS

Ringneck pheasants are suitable as pets. They can be kept in a chicken house and can be raised pretty much like chickens. They are often raised and released for hunting purposes. They can be fed the same diet as chickens, and if tame they can be allowed to range freely and will return to the safety of the chicken house to roost at night.

Special precautions need to be taken to make sure that none of their enemies can attack the in the chicken house.

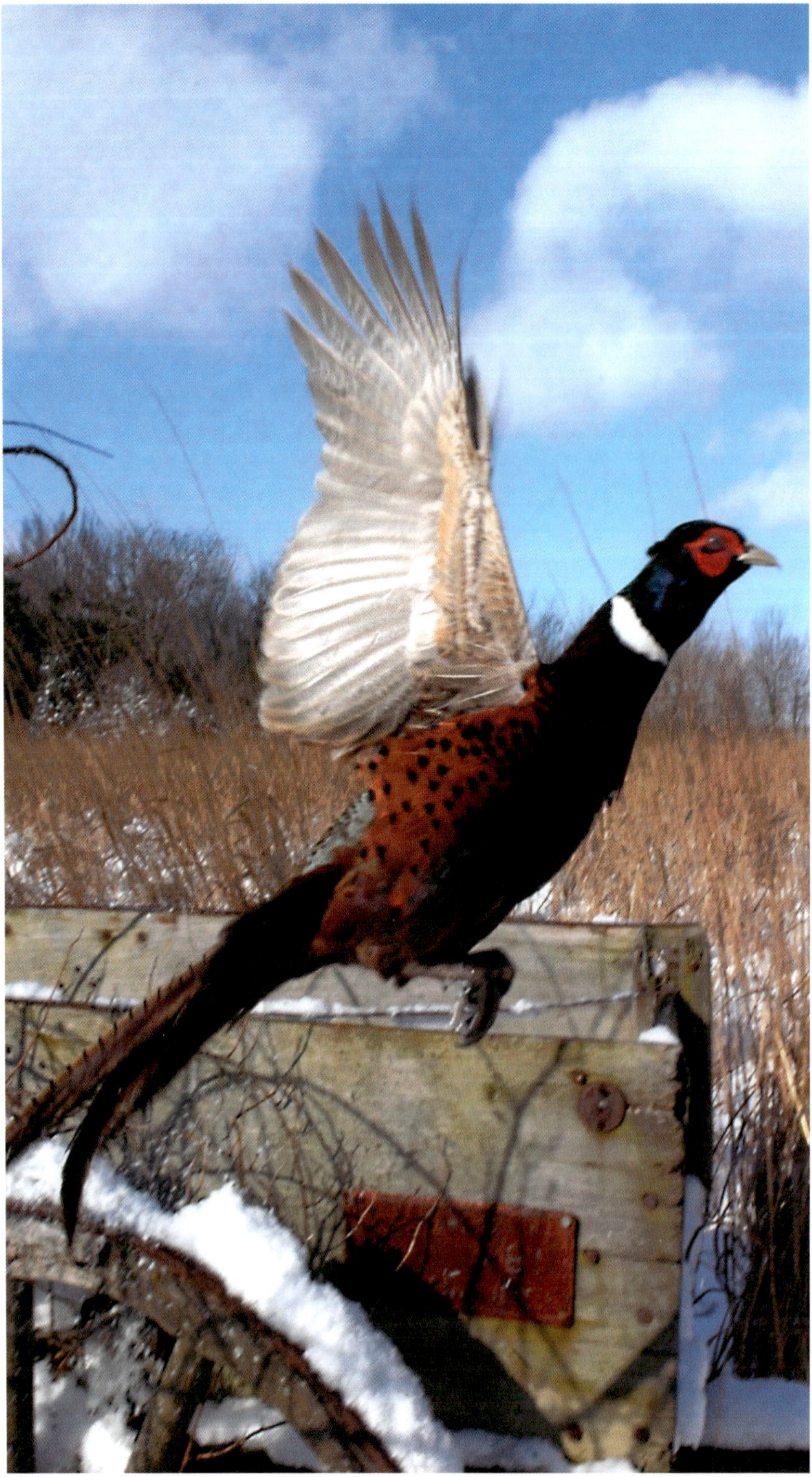

COLOR ME

COLOR ME

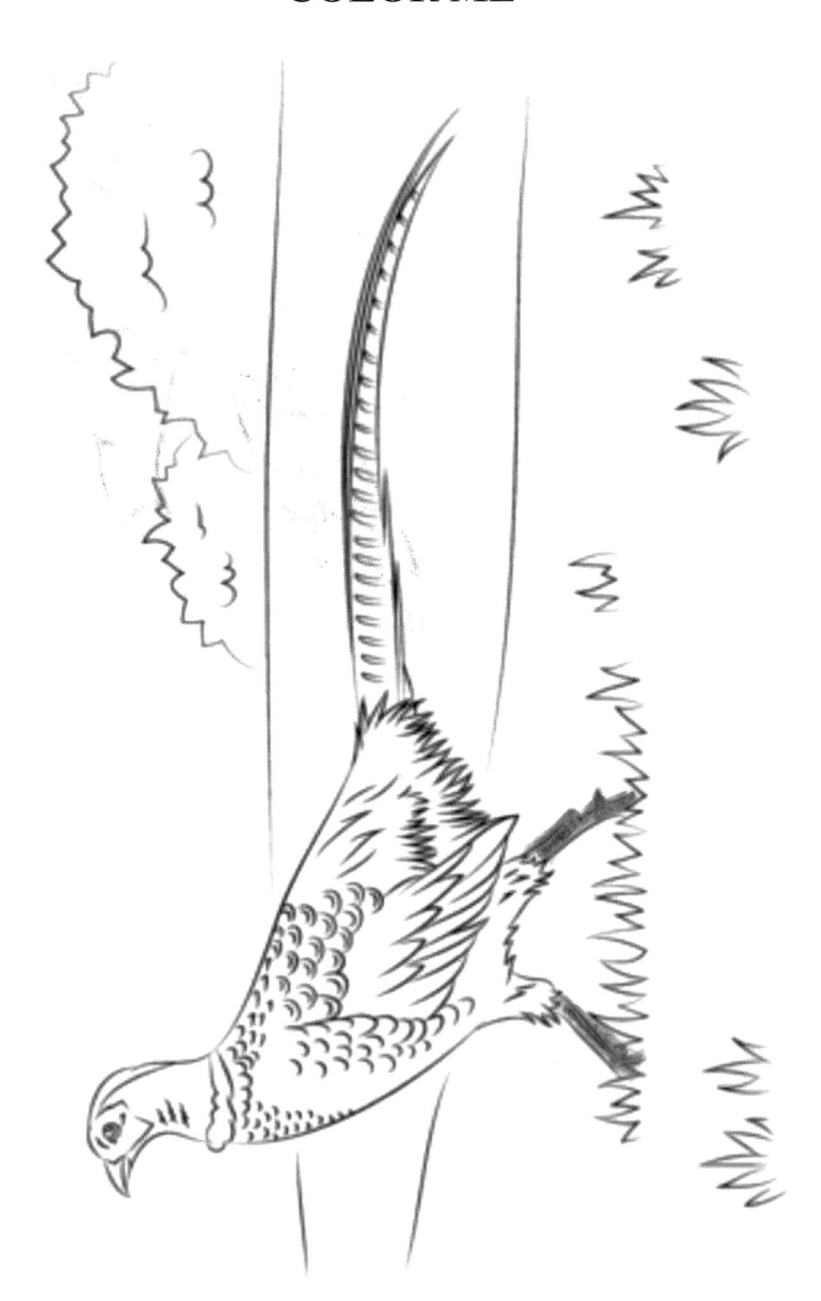

COLOR ME

COLOR ME

30

COLOR ME

COLOR ME

COLOR ME

COLOR ME

34

COLOR ME

COLOR ME

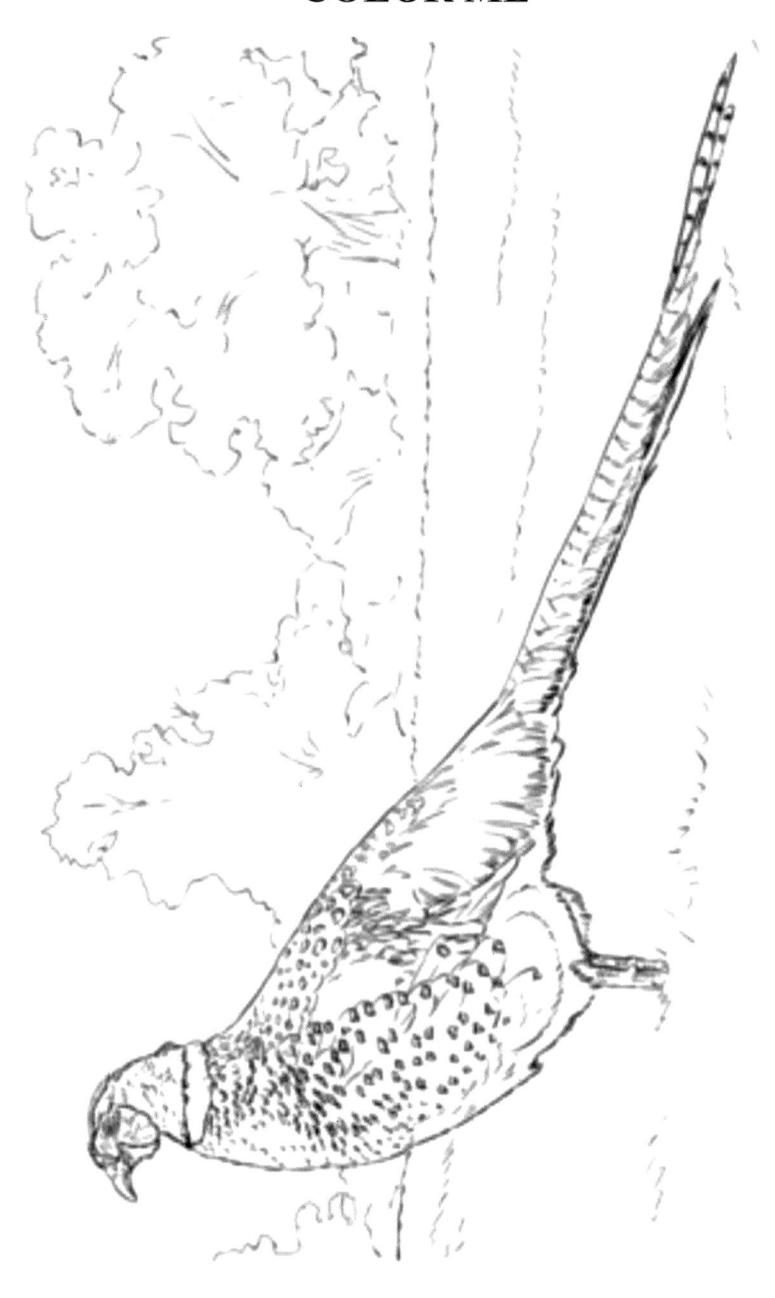

Please leave me a review here:

http://lisastrattin.com/Review-Vol-134

For more Kindle Downloads Visit **Lisa Strattin Author Page** on Amazon Author Central

http://amazon.com/author/lisastrattin

To see upcoming titles, visit my website at LisaStrattin.com– all books available on kindle!

http://lisastrattin.com

RINGNECK PHEASANT PHOTO

You can get one by copying and pasting this link into your browser:

http://lisastrattin.com/ringneckpheasantphoto

MONTHLY SURPRISE BOX

Get yours by copying and pasting this link into your browser

http://KidCraftsByLisa.com

Printed in Great Britain
by Amazon